MAD LIBS JUNIOR™

UNDER THE SEA MAD LIBS JUNIOR

By Roger Price and Leonard Stern

PSS!

PRICE STERN SLOAN

ISBN 978-0-8431-1350-1

11 13 15 14 12

MAD LIBS ⊙ JUNIOR
INSTRUCTIONS

MAD LIBS JUNIOR™ is a game for kids who don't like games!
It can be played by one, two, three, four, or forty.

RIDICULOUSLY SIMPLE DIRECTIONS:

At the top of each page in this book, you will find four columns of words, each headed by a symbol. Each symbol represents a part of speech. The symbols are:

★   ⊙   →   ?

NOUNS   ADJECTIVES   VERBS   MISC.

MAD LIBS JUNIOR™ is fun to play with friends, but you can also play it by yourself! To begin, look at the story on the page below. When you come to a blank space in the story, look at the symbol that appears underneath. Then find the same symbol on this page and pick a word that appears below the symbol. Put that word in the blank space, and cross out the word, so you don't use it again. Continue doing this throughout the story until you've filled in all the spaces. Finally, read your story aloud and laugh!

EXAMPLE:

"Good-bye!" he said, as he jumped into his _____ and _____
                        ?   →

off with his pet _____ .
            ★

★ NOUNS	⊙ ADJECTIVES	→ VERBS	? MISC.
car	curly	drove	hamster
boat	purple	~~danced~~	dog
roller skate	wet	drank	cat
taxicab	tired	twirled	~~giraffe~~
~~surfboard~~	silly	swam	monkey

"Good-bye!" he said, as he jumped into his __SURFBOARD__ and __DANCED__
                                ★   →

off with his pet __GIRAFFE__ .
        ?

In case you haven't learned about the parts of speech yet, here is a quick lesson:

A **NOUN** ✦ is the name of a person, place, or thing. *Sidewalk, umbrella, bathtub,* and *roller blades* are nouns.

An **ADJECTIVE** ☺ describes a person, place, or thing. *Lumpy, soft, ugly, messy,* and *short* are adjectives.

A **VERB** ➜ is an action word. *Run, jump,* and *swim* are verbs.

MISC. ? can be any word at all. Some examples of a word that could be miscellaneous are: *nose, monkey, five,* and *blue.*

MAD LIBS JUNIOR™ is fun to play with friends, but you can also play it by yourself! To begin, look at the story on the page below. When you come to a blank space in the story, look at the symbol that appears underneath. Then find the same symbol on this page and pick a word that appears below the symbol. Put that word in the blank space, and cross out the word, so you don't use it again. Continue doing this throughout the story until you've filled in all the spaces. Finally, read your story aloud and laugh!

PURPLE BEARD'S TREASURE

★ NOUNS	😊 ADJECTIVES	➡ VERBS	? MISC.
grapes	scary	wiggle	leg
pearls	smelly	read	nose
gum balls	funny	laugh	ear
coins	nice	yell	arm
mushrooms	silly	dance	finger
candles	weird	scream	tongue
onions	cool	skip	head
ribbons	little	giggle	hand
rubies	gross	cry	foot
meatballs	awesome	sneeze	toe
socks	stinky	sing	eye
diamonds	fancy	bark	knee

MAD LIBS JUNIOR

PURPLE BEARD'S TREASURE

Everyone knows that Purple Beard was a really _____ pirate.

He had a big purple beard and a wooden peg for a/an _____. **?**

He also had a parrot that would sit on his _____ and **?**

_____. Purple Beard stole from every ship on the sea. He

would put _____ in his beard and start to _____

whenever he boarded another ship. The people onboard thought Purple

Beard was so _____ that they'd _____ and hand

over all their _____. Years later when his treasure was

discovered, there was over a million dollars worth of _____.

What a/an _____ find!

MAD LIBS JUNIOR™ is fun to play with friends, but you can also play it by yourself! To begin, look at the story on the page below. When you come to a blank space in the story, look at the symbol that appears underneath. Then find the same symbol on this page and pick a word that appears below the symbol. Put that word in the blank space, and cross out the word, so you don't use it again. Continue doing this throughout the story until you've filled in all the spaces. Finally, read your story aloud and laugh!

KINDS OF SHARKS

★ NOUNS	☺ ADJECTIVES	→ VERBS	? MISC.
lemon	nice	read	eyes
hammer	silly	swim	ears
pretzel	smelly	wiggle	teeth
jellyfish	goofy	eat	ribs
pickle	crazy	dance	feet
steak	slippery	hunt	elbows
pinecone	pointy	yell	arms
octopus	spiky	bathe	legs
lollipop	scary	juggle	lips
tire	cuddly	skip	nostrils
horseshoe	skinny	sing	eyebrows
gumdrop	wacky	play	fingers

MAD LIBS JUNIOR
KINDS OF SHARKS

Sharks are really _____ creatures. There are lots of

_____ kinds of sharks. One kind is the _____

shark. This type of shark likes to _____ in warm, shallow

water. It is well-known for its _____ _____. Another

interesting kind of shark is the _____ head shark. In addition

to its _____ head, this unusual shark has _____-

shaped _____ and _____ _____.

Another kind of shark is the _____ shark, often considered

the deadliest. Its favorite meal is a nice, juicy _____, but

sometimes it bites people. If you see one coming toward you, start to

_____ as quickly as you can!

MAD LIBS JUNIOR™ is fun to play with friends, but you can also play it by yourself! To begin, look at the story on the page below. When you come to a blank space in the story, look at the symbol that appears underneath. Then find the same symbol on this page and pick a word that appears below the symbol. Put that word in the blank space, and cross out the word, so you don't use it again. Continue doing this throughout the story until you've filled in all the spaces. Finally, read your story aloud and laugh!

DOLPHIN SHOW

★	☺	➜	?
NOUNS	**ADJECTIVES**	**VERBS**	**MISC.**
tuba	bad	speak	ear
monkey	smelly	read	forehead
watermelon	fun	dance	mouth
seal	boring	paint	nose
TV	wacky	count	chin
oyster	wild	cook	belly
pumpkin	silly	sew	neck
rooster	goofy	laugh	tooth
cactus	weird	sing	cheek
killer whale	wet	write	eye
bowling ball	stinky	talk	back
shark	crazy	spell	lip

MAD LIBS JUNIOR
DOLPHIN SHOW

For my birthday, my parents wanted to get me a really _____

surprise, so they took me to the _____ show at Ocean Land.

We sat right in the front row, and my parents got me a big foam hat in

the shape of a/an _____. The star of the show was a

_____ dolphin named Winky who could balance a/an

_____ on her _____. Winky was really smart, and

she could even _____. Because it was my birthday, the

trainer had Winky give me a kiss on my _____. The dolphin

show was really _____. Next year for my birthday, I think I'll

just ask for a/an _____!

MAD LIBS JUNIOR™ is fun to play with friends, but you can also play it by yourself! To begin, look at the story on the page below. When you come to a blank space in the story, look at the symbol that appears underneath. Then find the same symbol on this page and pick a word that appears below the symbol. Put that word in the blank space, and cross out the word, so you don't use it again. Continue doing this throughout the story until you've filled in all the spaces. Finally, read your story aloud and laugh!

THE SEA CUCUMBER

★	😊	➡	?
NOUNS	**ADJECTIVES**	**VERBS**	**MISC.**
potato	slimy	tickle	eye
football	yummy	grab	tongue
dog	slippery	squeeze	brain
breadstick	mushy	eat	liver
log	squishy	bite	ear
slug	rubbery	lick	mouth
trumpet	gooey	poke	elbow
lollipop	puffy	rub	stomach
pillow	wet	slide	neck
peanut	foamy	waddle	heart
balloon	lumpy	pedal	forehead
noodle	cute	sniff	throat

The sea cucumber is not a vegetable; it's a _____ ☺ creature

that lives in the ocean. A sea cucumber looks kind of like a big

_____ _____ ★ . It's not a very smart creature ☺

and doesn't have a very big _____ ? . It likes to _____ ➡

its food, but it doesn't do much else. However, there's one really

_____ ☺ fact about the sea cucumber: If another creature tries

to _____ ➡ it, it shoots its _____ ? out of its

_____ ? . What a _____ ☺ mess! So remember,

if you ever meet a sea cucumber, don't try to _____ ➡ or

_____ ➡ it!

MAD LIBS JUNIOR™ is fun to play with friends, but you can also play it by yourself! To begin, look at the story on the page below. When you come to a blank space in the story, look at the symbol that appears underneath. Then find the same symbol on this page and pick a word that appears below the symbol. Put that word in the blank space, and cross out the word, so you don't use it again. Continue doing this throughout the story until you've filled in all the spaces. Finally, read your story aloud and laugh!

HOW TO CATCH AN OCTOPUS

★	☺	→	?
NOUNS	**ADJECTIVES**	**VERBS**	**MISC.**
potato chips	sneaky	dance	arms
jelly beans	sleepy	read	lips
snails	quick	sleep	brains
rubber bands	clever	cry	eyebrows
peaches	crazy	relax	legs
peanuts	smart	squirm	eyes
worms	silly	sneeze	fingers
pretzels	brave	sing	ears
sardines	quiet	giggle	mouths
lobsters	wacky	snort	feet
lemons	weird	hiccup	toes
cookies	wild	scream	teeth

MAD LIBS JUNIOR
HOW TO CATCH AN OCTOPUS

If you are _____ enough to think you can catch an octopus,

here are some _____ hints to help with your hunt:

1. You'll have to be very _____ to catch an octopus.

   Remember: They have eight _____!

2. Know where to look. An octopus is a very _____ creature

   that likes to hide in dark places where it can _____

   and _____.

3. Take some octopus bait. Their favorite snacks are _____

   and fish _____.

4. If an octopus latches on to you and won't let go, try to

   _____. Its _____ will get tired sooner or later.

MAD LIBS JUNIOR™ is fun to play with friends, but you can also play it by yourself! To begin, look at the story on the page below. When you come to a blank space in the story, look at the symbol that appears underneath. Then find the same symbol on this page and pick a word that appears below the symbol. Put that word in the blank space, and cross out the word, so you don't use it again. Continue doing this throughout the story until you've filled in all the spaces. Finally, read your story aloud and laugh!

LITTLE SPLASHY

★ NOUNS	☺ ADJECTIVES	➡ VERBS	❓ MISC.
shark	brave	sing	brain
cupcake	silly	giggle	heart
toilet	muddy	sneeze	tooth
pickle	crazy	dance	throat
crab	scared	cry	face
boat	goofy	jump	mouth
seahorse	weird	wiggle	elbow
log	smelly	hum	chin
starfish	squishy	scream	head
pineapple	cranky	weep	beard
guppy	rotten	cough	nose
clam	sad	shake	belly

My favorite movie is _____ *Little Splashy*. It's about a

_____ named Little Splashy who gets lost in the ocean. Along

the way, he meets his best friend, a _____ _____

named Buddy. At one point, Buddy and Splashy get kidnapped by an evil

_____ named "_____ _____" who

stuffs them into a giant clamshell. But Splashy is _____, and he

has a big _____. He starts to _____, and the

clamshell opens, setting them free. The ending of the movie is really

_____. Splashy finally finds his mother, who's so happy to see

him again that she starts to _____. I think _____

Little Splashy is my favorite movie ever. I even liked it better than *Moby*

_____!

MAD LIBS JUNIOR™ is fun to play with friends, but you can also play it by yourself! To begin, look at the story on the page below. When you come to a blank space in the story, look at the symbol that appears underneath. Then find the same symbol on this page and pick a word that appears below the symbol. Put that word in the blank space, and cross out the word, so you don't use it again. Continue doing this throughout the story until you've filled in all the spaces. Finally, read your story aloud and laugh!

THE GIANT SQUID

★ NOUNS	☺ ADJECTIVES	→ VERBS	? MISC.
hot dogs	squishy	talk	fingers
beaks	smelly	sing	lips
elephants	nice	laugh	arms
balloons	weird	swim	knees
whales	mushy	hiccup	eyes
tentacles	gentle	giggle	legs
carrots	playful	dance	ears
pancakes	goofy	sleep	feet
UFOs	stinky	play	eyelashes
clams	silly	gossip	mouths
green beans	soft	Rollerblade	teeth
aliens	friendly	ski	eyebrows

The giant squid is a creature with _____ **?** over thirty feet long.

Long ago, sailors thought the giant squid was a _____ sea

monster that would attack their boats and eat their _____.

Today, scientists know that these _____ creatures are not

monsters at all. They also know that the giant squid likes to

_____ and _____ and eats mostly _____.

Giant squid also have _____ **?** the size of large

_____. Imagine seeing that while you are swimming! Giant

squid are very _____ animals, but just be sure to steer clear of

their _____ **?**. Otherwise, they may start to _____!

MAD LIBS JUNIOR™ is fun to play with friends, but you can also play it by yourself! To begin, look at the story on the page below. When you come to a blank space in the story, look at the symbol that appears underneath. Then find the same symbol on this page and pick a word that appears below the symbol. Put that word in the blank space, and cross out the word, so you don't use it again. Continue doing this throughout the story until you've filled in all the spaces. Finally, read your story aloud and laugh!

JELLYFISH

★ NOUNS	😊 ADJECTIVES	→ VERBS	? MISC.
jelly	cold	lick	ear
ketchup	bad	bite	tongue
cheese	awesome	sniff	arm
ice	painful	pinch	body
noodles	slimy	poke	foot
hand lotion	cool	rub	leg
pudding	awful	hug	mouth
coffee	squishy	sting	head
rubber bands	gooey	jump	lip
ice cream	horrible	tickle	belly
sponges	mushy	kiss	eye
peanut butter	smelly	grab	hand

MAD LIBS JUNIOR
JELLYFISH

Jellyfish can make a day at the beach really _____. That's

because a jellyfish can _____ you while you're swimming and

leave a/an _____ mark on your body. The jellyfish is a/an

_____ animal that has stinging glands in its _____.

It gets its name because its body is the same texture as _____.

And believe it or not, in some parts of the world, people eat these

_____ creatures. They are usually served over

_____. If you ever get a jellyfish sting, be sure to put your

_____ in a bucket of _____. In just a few minutes,

the sting will start feeling _____.

From Under the Sea Mad Libs Junior™ • Copyright 2005 by Price Stern Sloan,
a division of Penguin Young Readers Group, 345 Hudson Street, New York, NY 10014.

MAD LIBS JUNIOR™ is fun to play with friends, but you can also play it by yourself! To begin, look at the story on the page below. When you come to a blank space in the story, look at the symbol that appears underneath. Then find the same symbol on this page and pick a word that appears below the symbol. Put that word in the blank space, and cross out the word, so you don't use it again. Continue doing this throughout the story until you've filled in all the spaces. Finally, read your story aloud and laugh!

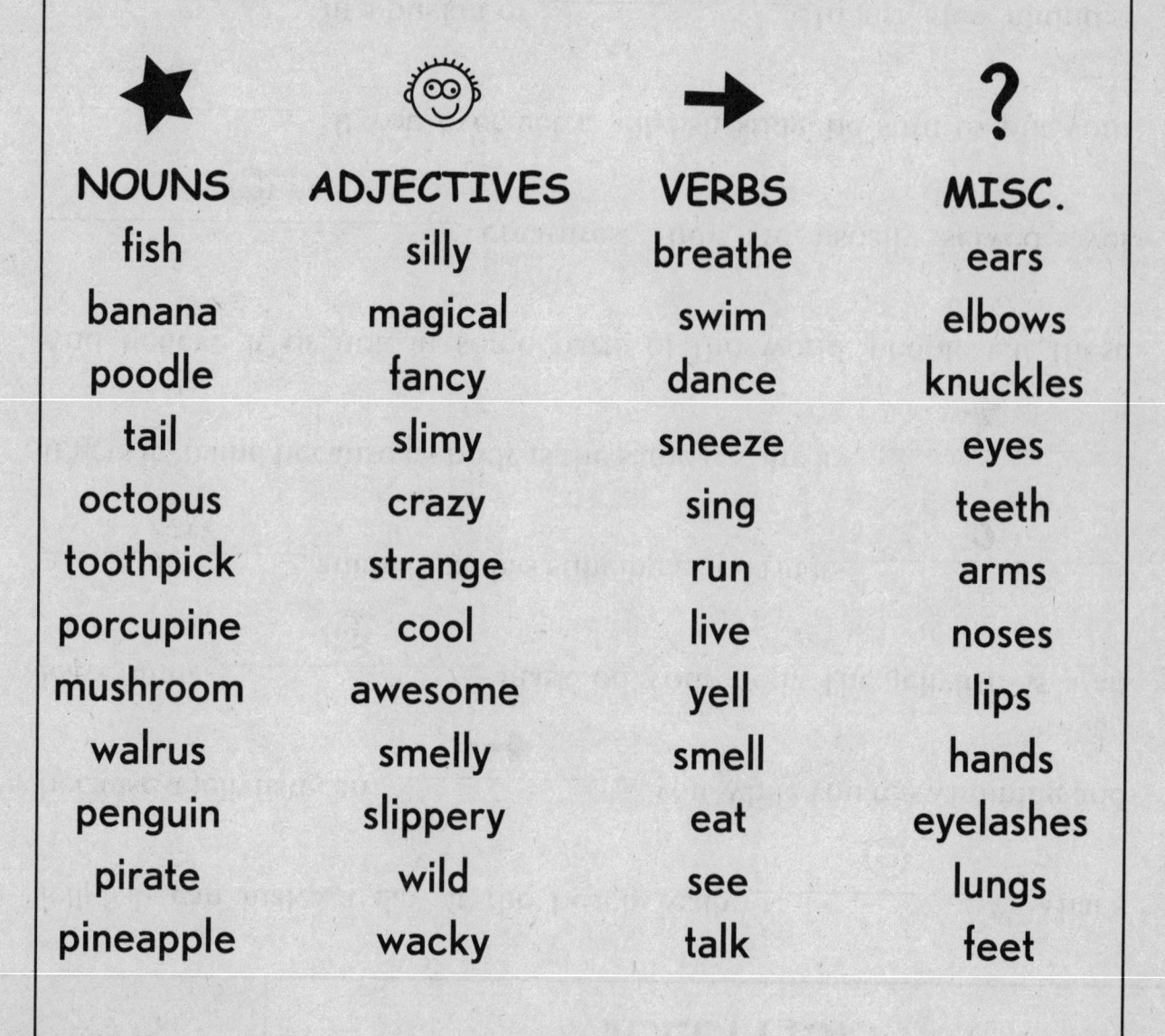

THE LEGEND OF THE MERMAID

★ NOUNS	☺ ADJECTIVES	→ VERBS	? MISC.
fish	silly	breathe	ears
banana	magical	swim	elbows
poodle	fancy	dance	knuckles
tail	slimy	sneeze	eyes
octopus	crazy	sing	teeth
toothpick	strange	run	arms
porcupine	cool	live	noses
mushroom	awesome	yell	lips
walrus	smelly	smell	hands
penguin	slippery	eat	eyelashes
pirate	wild	see	lungs
pineapple	wacky	talk	feet

MAD LIBS JUNIOR

THE LEGEND OF THE MERMAID

Legends say that mermaids are _____ sea creatures who are

half _____ and half _____. Mermaids are said to

have large _____ and _____ that are covered with

_____ scales. These help them to _____ underwater.

Legends say that mermaids have _____ powers. One of these

is that they can _____ with their eyes closed. There have also

been reports of a mermaid saving a shipwrecked _____ from

drowning. Even though most people think mermaids are

_____ creatures of fantasy, some people claim they are real.

They say the only reason we don't see more mermaids is because

mermaids can't _____ when they're on dry land.

MAD LIBS JUNIOR™ is fun to play with friends, but you can also play it by yourself! To begin, look at the story on the page below. When you come to a blank space in the story, look at the symbol that appears underneath. Then find the same symbol on this page and pick a word that appears below the symbol. Put that word in the blank space, and cross out the word, so you don't use it again. Continue doing this throughout the story until you've filled in all the spaces. Finally, read your story aloud and laugh!

SWIMMING WITH STINGRAYS

★ NOUNS	☺ ADJECTIVES	➡ VERBS	? MISC.
tissues	rubbery	hug	hands
olives	stinky	lick	ears
airplanes	squishy	taste	eyeballs
pancakes	smelly	cuddle	lips
mushrooms	slimy	tickle	teeth
fish	soft	grab	arms
cookies	mushy	squeeze	ribs
waffles	floppy	eat	feet
cotton balls	slippery	bite	elbows
grapes	foamy	kiss	armpits
potato chips	smooth	poke	nostrils
socks	puffy	sniff	fingers

MAD LIBS JUNIOR
SWIMMING WITH STINGRAYS

On vacation, my mom and I rented _____ wet suits and

went swimming with stingrays. Stingrays have large _____

_____ on either side of their bodies, and they like to

_____ fish. Stingrays are gray on top and white on the bottom,

and their _____ feel just like wet _____. They are

gentle, _____ creatures that look like big _____

_____. The stingrays ate some _____ right out of

my _____. One of the stingrays tried to _____ my

mom's _____ to eat her _____! But don't worry,

stingrays won't sting you or even _____ you, unless you

scare them.

MAD LIBS JUNIOR™ is fun to play with friends, but you can also play it by yourself! To begin, look at the story on the page below. When you come to a blank space in the story, look at the symbol that appears underneath. Then find the same symbol on this page and pick a word that appears below the symbol. Put that word in the blank space, and cross out the word, so you don't use it again. Continue doing this throughout the story until you've filled in all the spaces. Finally, read your story aloud and laugh!

THE FIRST SEA CREATURES

★	☺	→	?
NOUNS	**ADJECTIVES**	**VERBS**	**MISC.**
fins	scaly	talk	wrists
whales	slimy	dance	cheeks
school buses	nasty	breathe	toes
apples	bumpy	live	teeth
flippers	sticky	eat	lungs
frogs	spiny	sing	ears
toothpicks	creepy	swim	lips
lollipops	strange	juggle	palms
horses	odd	sleep	fingers
mice	weird	drive	knees
cupcakes	spiky	sneeze	eyes
elephants	mushy	growl	thighs

Long ago, in the time of the dinosaurs, there were _____

creatures that lived in the sea. These were the first sea creatures to ever

_____ in the water. Most of them were about the size of

_____. They were covered in _____ skin and had

large _____ that helped them _____ underwater.

These _____ creatures ate about three hundred pounds

of _____ a day (equal to the weight of one hundred

_____). They would catch food in their _____

_____ and use their _____ to eat it. Most

people believe these _____ creatures died thousands of years

ago, but some people say they still _____ deep in the ocean.

MAD LIBS JUNIOR™ is fun to play with friends, but you can also play it by yourself! To begin, look at the story on the page below. When you come to a blank space in the story, look at the symbol that appears underneath. Then find the same symbol on this page and pick a word that appears below the symbol. Put that word in the blank space, and cross out the word, so you don't use it again. Continue doing this throughout the story until you've filled in all the spaces. Finally, read your story aloud and laugh!

FISHING WITH GRANDPA

★ NOUNS	☺ ADJECTIVES	→ VERBS	? MISC.
french fries	gross	wiggle	head
minnows	stinky	splash	wrist
sardines	super	shake	elbow
mushrooms	tasty	dance	nose
onions	yummy	sneeze	knee
crickets	yucky	cry	belly
tails	delicious	shiver	mouth
green beans	good	talk	tooth
worms	cool	growl	foot
pretzels	nice	jiggle	ear
eggs	weird	jump	eye
hot dogs	crazy	skip	lip

I love to _____ ➡ with my grandpa! Yesterday he showed up

with his fishing hat on his _____ **?** and a big bucket full of

_____ ★ for bait. "The fish sure will think these are

_____ 🙂 !" said Grandpa. Grandpa also brought some

_____ ★ for him and me to snack on. Grandpa showed me

how to cast. "It's all in the _____ **?** ," he said. After a long time,

my fishing pole started to _____ ➡ . I reeled in a huge fish with

a great big _____ **?** ."That sure would be _____ 🙂 fried

up with some _____ ★ . Mmmm, Mmm," Grandpa said. But then

the fish started to _____ ➡ ! I felt _____ 🙂 , so I threw

it back in the water.

MAD LIBS JUNIOR™ is fun to play with friends, but you can also play it by yourself! To begin, look at the story on the page below. When you come to a blank space in the story, look at the symbol that appears underneath. Then find the same symbol on this page and pick a word that appears below the symbol. Put that word in the blank space, and cross out the word, so you don't use it again. Continue doing this throughout the story until you've filled in all the spaces. Finally, read your story aloud and laugh!

PUFFER FISH

★ NOUNS	☺ ADJECTIVES	→ VERBS	? MISC.
coconut	spiky	dance	ears
elephant	slimy	shake	arms
whale	puffy	scream	lips
dumpling	silly	sneeze	eyes
tuba	lumpy	jump	knuckles
walrus	slippery	giggle	fingers
igloo	shiny	sweat	spines
moose	weird	hop	feet
hippo	chewy	blink	teeth
pumpkin	hairy	twitch	toes
cactus	squishy	skate	cheeks
dinosaur	rubbery	yell	knees

The puffer _____, or blowfish, is a really _____

kind of fish. Puffer fish have really _____ _____

and big _____. When a puffer fish sees a/an _____,

it gets scared. Then it starts to _____ and blows itself up. If it's

really scared, it can puff up to the size of a/an _____! In some

parts of the world, people eat puffer fish _____ for dinner. But

diners must be careful, because the puffer fish's _____ are

very poisonous. One bite could make you _____ until you

turn blue. I think I'd rather eat a _____ _____!

MAD LIBS JUNIOR™ is fun to play with friends, but you can also play it by yourself! To begin, look at the story on the page below. When you come to a blank space in the story, look at the symbol that appears underneath. Then find the same symbol on this page and pick a word that appears below the symbol. Put that word in the blank space, and cross out the word, so you don't use it again. Continue doing this throughout the story until you've filled in all the spaces. Finally, read your story aloud and laugh!

SUPER SUBMARINE RIDE

★	☺	➡	?
NOUNS	**ADJECTIVES**	**VERBS**	**MISC.**
octopus	giant	run	feet
dolphin	slimy	yell	earlobes
torpedo	smelly	dance	eyebrows
clam	fun	shake	lips
crab	shiny	bounce	shoulders
banana	goofy	cry	teeth
jellyfish	cool	sing	toes
computer	wiggly	bark	fingers
sea lion	pretty	jump	elbows
lobster	silly	squeal	knees
whale	stinky	giggle	knuckles
potato	weird	snort	nostrils

MAD LIBS JUNIOR

SUPER SUBMARINE RIDE

At the Super Sea Park, my brother and I love to _____ ➡ on the

Super _____ 😊 Submarine Ride. The submarine is shaped a

like big metal _____ ⭐, and the seats are shaped like

_____ ❓. Before you get on, you have to make sure your

_____ ❓ reach the line on a sign out front. Last time, our little

sister started to _____ ➡ like a/an _____ ⭐ when they

told her she was too small. Once you're on, the _____ 😊

submarine first stops near a big _____ ⭐ that wiggles its

_____ ❓. But my favorite part is when the giant

_____ ⭐ starts to _____ ➡ and _____ ➡

when it sees the submarine. What a _____ 😊 ride!

MAD LIBS JUNIOR™ is fun to play with friends, but you can also play it by yourself! To begin, look at the story on the page below. When you come to a blank space in the story, look at the symbol that appears underneath. Then find the same symbol on this page and pick a word that appears below the symbol. Put that word in the blank space, and cross out the word, so you don't use it again. Continue doing this throughout the story until you've filled in all the spaces. Finally, read your story aloud and laugh!

HOW A PEARL IS MADE

★ NOUNS	😊 ADJECTIVES	➡ VERBS	? MISC.
sand	shiny	sing	eye
gold	slimy	laugh	ear
cheese	squishy	cry	tooth
dirt	beautiful	wiggle	toe
onion	weird	shake	mouth
metal	crazy	dance	belly button
chocolate	sick	spit	lip
popcorn	cool	yell	stomach
wood	gooey	fall	throat
chicken	slippery	skip	nose
pie	thick	choke	cheek
sugar	lumpy	scream	lung

MAD LIBS ☺ JUNIOR™
HOW A PEARL IS MADE

A real string of pearls is _____ enough to make anyone

_____. But did you know that pearls are made by

_____ creatures called oysters? It's true! It happens when a

piece of _____ gets into an oyster's _____. The

strange object makes the oyster feel _____, and it starts to

_____. This causes a _____ fluid to come out of

the oyster's _____. The object turns _____ like a

piece of _____, and it becomes a pearl. A pearl about the size

of your _____ might be worth even more than a pound of

_____! Isn't that _____?

MAD LIBS JUNIOR™ is fun to play with friends, but you can also play it by yourself! To begin, look at the story on the page below. When you come to a blank space in the story, look at the symbol that appears underneath. Then find the same symbol on this page and pick a word that appears below the symbol. Put that word in the blank space, and cross out the word, so you don't use it again. Continue doing this throughout the story until you've filled in all the spaces. Finally, read your story aloud and laugh!

DIRK DECKER DEEP-SEA DIVER

★ NOUNS	☺ ADJECTIVES	→ VERBS	? MISC.
surfboard	best	skiing	earlobes
necklace	worst	diving	shoulders
lobster	coolest	skating	muscles
gerbil	funniest	surfing	teeth
pear	scariest	singing	eyebrows
submarine	silliest	swimming	nostrils
painting	wildest	dancing	ears
diamond	smelliest	flying	elbows
monkey	goofiest	windsurfing	eyes
toothbrush	craziest	sneezing	lips
vase	neatest	sailing	knees
poodle	zaniest	Rollerblading	fingers

Dirk Decker Deep-Sea Diver is the _____ ☺ show on TV. Dirk is

always going to the _____ ☺ places in the world. Dirk has

really big _____ **?**, and he loves _____ ➡

and _____ ➡ crimes. My favorite episode was about a

_____ ★ that got stolen by some _____ ➡ pirates. The

_____ ☺ part was when Dirk caught the pirates. Can you

believe he captured them by _____ ➡ right into their

_____ ★ ? It was the _____ ☺ thing I have ever seen!

Dirk Decker's not afraid of anything, well, except _____ ➡ —

he's terrified of that!

MAD LIBS JUNIOR™ is fun to play with friends, but you can also play it by yourself! To begin, look at the story on the page below. When you come to a blank space in the story, look at the symbol that appears underneath. Then find the same symbol on this page and pick a word that appears below the symbol. Put that word in the blank space, and cross out the word, so you don't use it again. Continue doing this throughout the story until you've filled in all the spaces. Finally, read your story aloud and laugh!

GLASS-BOTTOM BOAT RIDE

★ NOUNS	☺ ADJECTIVES	➡ VERBS	? MISC.
dog	cool	tickle	fingers
pickle	weird	grab	eyeballs
lion	crazy	squeeze	ears
banana	silly	eat	teeth
chicken	smelly	bite	thumbs
hippo	goofy	lick	brains
angel	wacky	hug	lips
mushroom	awesome	rub	eyebrows
zebra	bubbly	run	nostrils
dinosaur	wild	waddle	eyelids
cupcake	exciting	nibble	toes
pony	fun	sniff	cheeks

A great way to see lots of _____ sea creatures is to take a ride

on a glass-bottom boat. I went on one with my _____ family

when we were on vacation. It's _____! You can put your

_____ right up to the glass on the bottom of the boat. You

?

feel so close to the fish that it looks like you could reach out and

_____ one. We saw one fish that looked like a giant

➡

_____ with big _____-looking _____.

★   **?**

But the best part was when a huge _____ fish started

★

wiggling its _____ and tried to _____ our boat.

?   **➡**

My dad was so scared that even his _____ were shaking!

?

MAD LIBS JUNIOR™ is fun to play with friends, but you can also play it by yourself! To begin, look at the story on the page below. When you come to a blank space in the story, look at the symbol that appears underneath. Then find the same symbol on this page and pick a word that appears below the symbol. Put that word in the blank space, and cross out the word, so you don't use it again. Continue doing this throughout the story until you've filled in all the spaces. Finally, read your story aloud and laugh!

BLUE WHALES

★ NOUNS	☺ ADJECTIVES	→ VERBS	? MISC.
school buses	slimy	barking	eyeballs
shrimp	small	wrestling	skin
goldfish	weird	singing	eyebrows
rockets	colorful	falling	fingers
dolphins	huge	swimming	lips
bananas	angry	dancing	noses
submarines	slippery	diving	knees
footballs	rubbery	laughing	toes
pickles	happy	reading	ears
blimps	goofy	howling	eyelashes
aliens	smelly	talking	tongues
hot dogs	greasy	squeezing	belly buttons

MAD LIBS ☺ JUNIOR
BLUE WHALES

Blue whales are really _____ creatures. They look like big

_____ _____ and can be over one hundred

_____ long. That's bigger than ten huge _____

lined up end to end. Blue whales get their name from their grayish-blue

_____. Blue whales enjoy _____ with other

whales underwater and can make unusual sounds with their

_____. Some scientists have even confused them for

_____ _____. Blue whales eat over seven

thousand pounds of _____ a day to give them energy for

_____. They don't have teeth. Instead, they have rows of tiny

_____ in their mouths that filter _____ out of the

water. Isn't that _____?

From Under the Sea Mad Libs Junior™ • Copyright 2005 by Price Stern Sloan,
a division of Penguin Young Readers Group, 345 Hudson Street, New York, NY 10014.

MAD LIBS JUNIOR™ is fun to play with friends, but you can also play it by yourself! To begin, look at the story on the page below. When you come to a blank space in the story, look at the symbol that appears underneath. Then find the same symbol on this page and pick a word that appears below the symbol. Put that word in the blank space, and cross out the word, so you don't use it again. Continue doing this throughout the story until you've filled in all the spaces. Finally, read your story aloud and laugh!

SCUBA DIVING LESSON

★ NOUNS	☺ ADJECTIVES	➡ VERBS	? MISC.
hams	crazy	dance	eyes
kittens	silly	sing	fingers
pillows	goofy	talk	knees
helicopters	funny	breathe	ears
boats	weird	chew	teeth
lizards	wacky	swim	lips
peanuts	nutty	jump	feet
noodles	slippery	skip	cheeks
anteaters	cool	giggle	nostrils
elephants	tough	juggle	hands
pumpkins	furry	cry	eyelids
gumdrops	strange	run	shoulders

MAD LIBS JUNIOR
SCUBA DIVING LESSON

My _____ dad and I decided to take a scuba diving lesson. I

was so excited that I threw on my bathing suit and started to

_____ ."I hope we see a big _____ shark!" I cried.

Our scuba instructor was a _____ guy with muscles as big as

_____ . He even had muscles on his _____ ! Dad

looked pretty _____ with his two flippers strapped to his

_____ . After an hour in the pool, Dad and I looked like two

wet _____ .I quickly realized that I wasn't going to see a shark

or any other _____ creature that day. Dad and I had to stay in

the pool until we learned how to _____ underwater!

MAD LIBS JUNIOR™ is fun to play with friends, but you can also play it by yourself! To begin, look at the story on the page below. When you come to a blank space in the story, look at the symbol that appears underneath. Then find the same symbol on this page and pick a word that appears below the symbol. Put that word in the blank space, and cross out the word, so you don't use it again. Continue doing this throughout the story until you've filled in all the spaces. Finally, read your story aloud and laugh!

SEA TURTLES

★	☺	→	?
NOUNS	ADJECTIVES	VERBS	MISC.
peanut	slippery	splashing	elbows
sock	crusty	dancing	wrists
magnet	squishy	singing	hands
tomato	tough	talking	eyes
gumdrop	hard	skiing	teeth
pin	crunchy	diving	shoulders
sponge	slimy	skating	lips
pretzel	floppy	sailing	feet
surfboard	hairy	snorkeling	fingernails
lemon	bony	laughing	toes
pea	lumpy	playing	ears
pickle	square	jumping	eyebrows

SEA TURTLES

Sea turtles are _____ turtles that spend most of their time

_____ and _____ in the sea. Sea turtles have four

huge _____ **?** that push them through the water like paddles.

And like other turtles, they have big _____ _____ **?**

that protect their bodies. There are many types of sea turtles, including the

_____ head and the _____ back. A female sea

turtle will lay about two hundred _____ eggs in the sand.

The baby sea turtles soon start _____ their _____ **?**

through their eggs to hatch. At first, they are only about the size of a

_____ , but they can grow up to six feet long!

MAD LIBS JUNIOR™ is fun to play with friends, but you can also play it by yourself! To begin, look at the story on the page below. When you come to a blank space in the story, look at the symbol that appears underneath. Then find the same symbol on this page and pick a word that appears below the symbol. Put that word in the blank space, and cross out the word, so you don't use it again. Continue doing this throughout the story until you've filled in all the spaces. Finally, read your story aloud and laugh!

TIDE POOLS

★ NOUNS	☺ ADJECTIVES	➡ VERBS	? MISC.
snails	wet	find	eyes
marbles	funny	eat	ears
sharks	small	tickle	teeth
plants	weird	pinch	knees
creatures	slippery	poke	lips
animals	cool	hug	nostrils
stars	gross	kiss	elbows
monkeys	lovely	squeeze	legs
unicorns	squishy	bite	earlobes
bugs	neat	lick	eyebrows
pumpkins	smelly	sniff	fingers
worms	squiggly	grab	toes

There are lots of _____ things to see in a tide pool! Tide pools

are small pools of seawater that are filled with tiny _____ and

_____. In the tide pool, these things are safe from big

_____ creatures that might _____ them if they

lived out in the ocean. My brother and I always play a game to see who

can _____ the most creatures in a tide pool. One time, I saw

some sea _____ with lots of little _____. I tried

to _____ them, and they squirted water at my

_____. That was really _____! But my brother

found really _____ things in the tide pool. He saw

hundreds of tiny _____ that tried to _____ his

_____!

This book is published by

PSS!

PRICE STERN SLOAN

whose other splendid titles include such literary classics as

Alphabet Mad Libs Junior™
Animals, Animals, Animals! Mad Libs Junior™
Once Upon a Mad Libs Junior™
Prehistoric Mad Libs Junior™
School Rules! Mad Libs Junior™
Scooby-Doo! Mad Libs Junior™
Snack Attack! Mad Libs Junior™
Sports Star Mad Libs Junior™
Summer Camp Mad Libs Junior™
Summer Fun Mad Libs Junior™
Super Silly Mad Libs Junior™

and many more!

Mad Libs® and Mad Libs Junior™ are available wherever books are sold.